DEC

ADE

NCE

Thuy On is an arts journalist, editor, critic, and poet. She's currently Reviews Editor and writer for online publication, ArtsHub. *Turbulence* (UWAP 2020) was her debut collection of poetry.

DECADENCE

THUY ON

UWA PUBLISHING

First published in 2022 by
UWA Publishing
Crawley, Western Australia 6009
www.uwap.uwa.edu.au

UWAP is an imprint of UWA Publishing
a division of The University of Western Australia

THE UNIVERSITY OF WESTERN AUSTRALIA

ISBN: 978-1-76080-207-3

NATIONAL LIBRARY OF AUSTRALIA A catalogue record for this
book is available from the
National Library of Australia

Cover design by Mika Tabata
Typeset in Joanna by Lasertype
Printed by Lightning Source

uwapublishing

Dedicated to decadent word wranglers, bibliophiles and practitioners of semicolons, and Oxford commas.

Contents

SPACES

META

26 soldiers

A small army pressed into service
from capline to baseline   .
marching smartly across the page
some with proud embellishments
on standard issue typeface
a swash here a serif there
tracking tightly in different formations
ablazed with wor(l)d building directives
trailing bullet points in their wake
                    & a single orphan.

Ceci n'est pas une poème!

No mad scatter of berets
flung around like frisbees
No beatnik finger clicking
in quasi groove time
No pretence of a saxophone slide
with your smooth diphthong
No midnight spoken word howling
to a nonchalant fat moon
No singing a love letter
to trees sentinel like a field of crosses
We don't want to hear words
as unhitched as train carriages
falling from your wine-bruised lips
and a heart as transparent as rice paper.

L'esprit de l'escalier

How many times have you succumbed
to the wit of the staircase
a belated retort on the way out?
prepared for Wildean whimsy
so sly of mouth smirk of face
but your coattails are caught on the door
your foot trips on a wobbly nail
more ripped than riposte
bon mots scattering
in freefall like broken marbles
across the lining floor.

Word slut

I'm so lascivious
I don't care which ones I go with
roll around with
those short nubby ones
the long elegant ones
the ones from a mongrel mixed race
that fit like rough marbles in your mouth
a bit of this at the front
a bit of that at the rear
polysyllables that jostle for equal attention
the everyday vanilla ones
and the special occasions
only used to impress
such oral delights
I like them every which way.

Grant me

Dear purveyor of written goods:
Please fill out your name, age, sex, address, race, pronouns.
Degree of psychic desperation.
In 500 words (min) double-spaced (Garamond) PDF (only), state why
you are better than the other pen-sweaty hordes and thus deserve our
largesse.

Are you
young
sexy
poor
humble
ethnic
outside the dominant patriarchal paradigm?
(Award yourself five points for each category you fulfil.)
Is there a squiggly line below your name in Microsoft Word? (Award
yourself ten points.)

Please work this out to the closest percentage: if the pie is worth
$200k and you're one of 39041 entries, what's the likelihood of your
gaining a crumb?
How large is your Twitter following? (don't lie, we have bot-detection
software.)

Have you ever used #amwriting to show everyone just how
productive you are?
Have you slept with or otherwise entered a mutually beneficial
relationship with any of the following: agents, publishers, editors,
publicists, bookseller, critics? (Why not? FFS, we can't do everything
for you!)

Insert the following in a single sentence less than 200 but more than 150 words: creativity, outside the square, exegesis, arts framework, own voices, future investment, strategy initiative, diversity, emerging.

Blurb yourself in the omniscient third person as though Tim Winton would have described you mid-surf just after he dodged a rip. Now do it in the second person as though Helen Garner was scribbling about you in her diary while in between husbands.

Name a writer from the following genres: rural noir, Scandi noir, Tartan noir and chick lit, chook lit, clit lit. (Bonus two points if your writing can feasibly be said to fall under any of these categories).

Do you think you can manage a pensive black-and-white, staring-into-the-middle-distance author picture? (This is a trick question. There's only one answer).

Sign here...and here... and here... to exempt us from damages, if perchance (unlikely, but you never know, hey?) you win (! insert crazy emoticon) and then have a minor breakdown for failing to live up to everyone's collective expectations with your sophomore work, thereby provoking the ire of right-wing columnists hissing about taxpayers money and sensitive petal, wanky artistes.

Go out on a full moon night and scream out "but the literary industry adds immeasurable value to the nation's economical and social capital."

In vino veritas

Watching men drink
too many times
drumming fingers
sudden fish of eye flash
wet-tongued hungry

in dull bar lighting
I can still read
their morphology of limbs
the perverted
Auslan patois

I'm the suffix
this body of text
to be uncoiled before them
never was the intention
for a novel-length affair

just a scattering tang
of syllables that taste
of short and sharp
and then thirst slaked
wilfully spittooned.

Lyrebird

You lyrebird
of borrowed sound

so lax
with your s y n
    t a x
ro mantic
pe
dantic
antics
faux
fall

twisting fəˈnɛtɪk tricks that
get stuck
in the uvula

your speakeasy box
a frequency so attuned

a caffeinated shock jock
to jolt into acquiescence

paroles paroles paroles

you think
you've riddled me out
a lure of honey

but I'm indissoluble
a sym m et r i c a l

I'm the dapple around a rustle
a treble clef before dancing notes

the play yet to be scripted
a story not yours to tell.

Bonsai clipped

I may seem like prose
the way I line things up
so punctilious
but I'm more poetry
bonsai-clipped
spaces   between
not easily parsed
I'm metaphor shaped
a cat sphinxed in shadow

a beat and then
some non sequiturs

this isn't chipped enamel
just cloud against blue
that's not diamond
just the sea breaking apart
it's not history
just a bite into cliff.

Sans

That letter was wounded
I shot the serif
the projection abutting
the smooth lines
an affront to the type
of face I wanted:
naked without
flourishes.

Dire Critics

Within this novel you've managed to
A) draw from a deep aquifer of emotions
B) elicit feeling as cold and dead as stars
C) master sarcasm as well as a millennial's emojis

Do you really believe that
A) each one of your books is sui generis?
B) your novel's architecture is not termite-riddled?
C) your themes aren't interred in confusion?

Your dialogue is
A) as pitch imperfect as nail on chalkboard
B) a vivisector's weapon
C) like hoiking phlegm on footpath

In terms of characterisation your protagonists are
A) as cloying as honeycomb
B) as bracing as painting en plein air
C) AI metallic in manner and feeling

The plot holes in your narrative are so wide they are
A) doll-legs akimbo
B) the distance from Saturn to the moon
C) phallic-cacti in the flat plains of a marathon runner.

Book Blurb Bingo

By golly it's rollicking this sweeping saga palaver you'll be a-weeping because coming of age is all the rage its luminosity is a ferocity a five-star recommended read in a single setting I'll be a-betting it's unputdownable cos it's of its time and place it'll be a crime if you miss it in your prime never less than assured the prose is stunning it's on the money c'mon I'll be gunning for this tour de force always on course such dialogue and diction in this auto fiction the colour of his face a betrayal of his race he's a consummate stylist you have to try it epic and prophetic shot through with fire frenetic but oh so lyrical a miracle covers all bases is sober in places this meditation on grief and loss a book you surely won't toss in the hands of a lesser writer the impact would be lighter but because it's a visual feast he didn't miss a beat so tender in such a slender volume on trend do lend it to your friend will dazzle your eyes (everyone dies!) he has a keen ear for voice a soft heart for place the skilful way he manages to lace such disparate threads so plot and character are wed this book will sear and melt the coldest heart this unflinching account will amount to instant classic the narrative flows the metaphor glows there's both highs and woes and hey the coal-eyed child will lose and find his way deepen his horizons but his home town will stay as tight-fisted ornery and small the zig-zagging past and present action won't pall a bildungsroman roaming all over the land the sweet purity of hope in every line a skip dance of poetry that's so silver gossamer fine and melded with stiletto wit it'll be a bestselling hit no wonder I'm flaunting it's so haunting so daunting you won't ever find such a poignant reflection will hold your attention across all of its sections this piece of perfection.

Dr/ink

A book worm is an ink drinker
coursing blue-black
that glides after the swallow of pages
sluicing through veins
with cellular efficiency

past plump organs
beating hard now after the ingestion
of vital words that break down
to morphemes
trace elements
of sustenance.

Get Lit

In the attic madwoman Bertha
is holding tight onto Dorian's portrait
In Pemberley Lizzy is wondering
whether to climb the hierarchical stairs.

The Beta-minuses are high on soma
the White Witch entices with rose water and sugar
the Joads can make do with just some
milk n' honey and maybe some oranges, thanks.

Boo's ghosting the midnight streets
the Proles are hanging out washing. Again.
Alice is tired of non-reflective looking glasses
and Jay just can't see beyond the green.

Domestic drudgery or a good sex life, Emma?
a whopping great marlin or your sanity, old man?
why don't you pick someone your own size, Humbert?
you should've eaten that damn cake already, Miss H.

Victor, your patchwork skills were seriously shoddy
Cathy & Heathcliff stfu about the blustery moors
Look inwards, you're the phoniest of them all, Holden
Just quietly Homer, a better title? *Monsters and Goddesses*

Up for breaking the time-space continuum, Miranda?
just imagine if telecommunications existed, Tess!
and really Marcel, whether or not dipped in lime blossom tea
madeleines just aren't that delicious or memorable.

Ex Libris

This book belongs to:

the reader
the critic
the interior decorator
who buys it from deceased estates
checking for ye olde spines
to furnish an apartment

the child
the superannuated
the teacher
who force feeds dead white males
to a vegan feminist collective

the numerically illiterate
the socially maladroit
the naif
who tries on a wardrobe
of different lives.

Errata

This life [insert list of errors]
I don't believe I did that
can we retract' can this bit be [redacted]?
[this too] [and this] [and chapters 4–8]
little slips of white paper please:
what ought be there instead
yes this man with a grin like the highway
a floof of brown hair
eyes that wear their kindness gently
soft and hard where it matters
can he amble on in early
not the penultimate scene
can I take the other one out?
are we able to do a Find and Replace with all mentions of him?
at the very least a transposition
also it's the wrong font all throughout
I need grace and gravitas to hold me up
Comic sans really? what the fuck?

Mask

What's with the masks?
your eyebrow-raised ask
why leather & lace
over the shapes of your face?
what's there to hide
can you really not abide
the nakedness unpainted?
must you be armoured and feinted
in your moves, a wary moat
island from me, cool and remote?

Dear Sir, I wear them not to bewitch
I'm not some cunning bitch
nor your dolly bird fingering
purloined plumage hindering
your rightful access
to truth's riotous mess
& your anatomising gaze
I preen them bold, unfazed
look beneath them should you dare
not artifice but art laid bare.

Water haiku x5

1. Rain sheeting down fast
vertiginous then flatten
slick rainbow puddles.

2. Fish gliding in sky?
those galaxies of grey
falcons swooping by.

3. Tin roof thunder clap
a startled slip, gaping skin
shards of dropped dishes.

4. Koi swimming upstream
gold and silver flashing bright
beating the currents.

5. You are blue whale eye
a gerund of editors
water in desert.

Revolution

By each day's revolution
there'll be music to jump the blood
heart-scalpel pages
that'll bleed their mark
the trickle of pen into flood
and you will sit in the halo of candlelight
this humble supplicant
to the overripe moon
and wait for the soft press of night.

Argot

1. The words are tadpoles
thrashing through the night
to break surface tension

2. Beware the portent of surliness
the cat tail question mark
swiping into exclamation

3. A detonation of adjectives
fireworks in the dark
clauses crackling into life

4. A villanelle in pretty refrain
twirling with five partners
dipping in and out of sight.

Why poetry?

1. Because you saw a weed pushing through the cracks and decide you need to create a whole iambic pentameter scaffold around this precious green metaphor of hope
2. Because psychologists are too expensive for bile and blood regurgitation
3. Because you met someone who needs to be immortalised before age dulls their eyes and cools your heat
4. Because you fancy yourself an eco-warrior as the world burns and drowns
5. Because society's done you wrong so instead of a thesis only your supervisor will read you shrinkwrap your consternation into a cinquain that two more people will read
6. Because you're into single page instant gratification
7. Because they don't allow line breaks and stanzas in letters to the editor
8. Because loneliness and sexual frustration need an outlet
9. Because you're lazy and don't want to story plot with 3 unreliable narrators and a past and present timeline that spans half a century
10. Because you want to make sure the pedants count out all the Haiku syllables.

Unclassified

The Dewey Decimal
so incontrovertible
exacting and immutable
yet a speck infinitesimal
is your life: random and intangible
where do you fit? There's no easy bind
Literature and Rhetoric 800–899?
as bookworm on pages you've fully dined?
The Arts 700–799?
verily your words unspool so fine
Languages 400–499?
sure why not you dare opine
Philosophy and Psychology 100–199?
well you do bang on about the daily grind
Religions 200–299?
no, to hell with divinekind
Technology 600-699?
ha! stuck on Android – already behind
History, Bio and Geography 900-999?
who you are & where you're going still yet to find
Natural Sciences and Maths 500–599?
with numbers you're loose & without spine
Social Sciences 300–399?
too many laws to render you blind
So General Works 001–099
in your own category undefined.

Murmuration

M
  M
    Mu
      Mur
        Murm
          M
          M
          Murm
            Murmur
            Murmur
              Murmura
              Murmura
              Murmura
              Murmura
                Murmuratio
                  Murmuratio
                    Murmuratio
                      Murmuration
                      Murmuration
                      Murmuration
                      Murmuration
                      Murmuration
                      Murmuratio
                      Murmaratio
                  Murmaratio
                  Murmaratio
                  Murmaratio
                Murmura
                Murmura
                Murmura
              Murmur
              Murmur
              Murmur
            Murm
          Murm
          Murm
          Murm
        Mur
        Mu
          M
            Murm
            Murm
            Murm
              Murmarat
                Murmurat
                  Murmuratio
                  Murmuratio
                    Murmuration
                    Murmuration

PHYSICAL

Ripe

Now when you eat a feijoa
lightly perfumed
creamy flesh
you'll think of me
the first time
collected from the lane
a stray in the dark
dropped sweet

Sorbet

I'm no phoneticist
but the roll of your name
in my devoted mouth
just a single syllable
ending in
the parting of lips
like a tingle of sorbet
your name is a neutraliser
sugar pills of magic
talisman against hurt
to breathe in and swallow.

Punctuated

You curl around me
open-ended and soft-backed
one half of a parenthesis.

Decadence

Lying on our side in concavity
spoon-nesting the warmth of skin
your breath on my shoulder
an idle arm draped like loose ribbon

two commas ,, an extra long pause —
after so much exertion there's respite
(we've just bracketed)
encircled one another

I don't want an ellipsis fade to black ...
but an arrest in time
or a backward space <--
to the first line in our story.

Buddha's Tears

Bellies warmed from stew
I'm cat lounging on you
the Buddha's tears have blossomed

a buzz of TV brightens
the dimmed room where
indolence is wallpaper

later: the cadence quickens
a gallop repositioning
flanks cooled and slick

outside the air nips
bites a crescent in the moon
a watery daub trailing streaks.

Williamstown Pier

We're walking in a painting
pointillist blue and silver
gold and light

white-masted boats
diagonally splayed
fanning the water

If only: Chagall lovers
breeze giddy
ripples below our feet

you're pulling me up:
kites kissing the sun
a slow rising melody.

Basal Ganglia

There'll be a bath
so it'll be a clean and dirty
day and night by the sea
when you'll take my mouth
to your own

will there be a view
outside our nest
this shimmer
an extension of your eye
a blue-grey vista?

framed against the window
a poem to Rodin:
marble that'll tremble
when you take my hand
in your own.

Symphony

Xylophonic tinkles across the water these gentle chimes on bobbing boats what rivulets of fate led us here tonight? Awed quiet at this gentle symphony of dark air and music the panorama so finely curated it could be an exhibition of balance the liquid horizontal the solid vertical and later cold to warmth the body of water domesticated to a bathtub the faraway city lights now a flickering candle a contraction from all the vastness of the world to just you opposite me forshortened and I can feel contentment filling me up like corpuscles in a vein and life is atomised to this very heartbeat.

Bird-boned

Tonight the sky was polished marble slab
when I drove home from you
no longer with bright red lipstick
as quietly radiant as the necklace of light
on the West Gate Bridge above

tonight I will sleep with the film of sweat
hair matted and skin tender
scrawled over with your invisible signature
warm from the exchanges of breath
& the motion of bodies through space

tonight the world feels a little less cruel
surely an agent of benediction not chaos
led me to you wild-eyed & bird-boned
that very first time a tremulous hope
caught in the throat awaiting expression.

White Pages

In pallid light
I saw the rise of your chest
in soft sleep profiled to me
your calligraphic body
curling up its lean lines
you're a palimpsest of all the lovers
who've ever pressed upon you
but this bed is white as a page
rumpled in repose but unmarked
waiting for us to take a pen each.

Wide Open Road

We should have played that Triffids song
on this fine wintry day
dipping in and out of the clouds

lemony sun through the windscreen
rolling down a dark ribbon
bisected by green

you're tapping your fingers
singing above the hum of engine
distant mountains beckoning

gradually and then suddenly
we're driving in the mist
I'm a new Romantic

bone-china
quicksilver soul
you're made of firmer music

and the beat pulses in our blood
like drumming underground
as we push into the fragile light.

Words for Friends

I knew by the way you
harnessed order
to occupy those squares
that we would be
friends for words
allies for the sport
of wrestling meaning
lovers for the placement
of connecting units
I knew I could trust
my hand in yours
that you can smooth flux
indulge a private code
the combinations
and permutations
only decipherable to us.

Mixed Media

The fluorescent ball hangs low and heavy
as though punctured by skyscrapers
fallen, it sits squat, burning

over a nursery of bobbing boats
lit in baby blue and pink pastels
rocked to sleep by tender waves

in the distance black swan smudges
in the foreground flickers like fire flies
on the pier respectful murmurings

and you and I? we're silent witnesses
a brief but significant layer
forming right now in our lives' crusts.

Lasso

You're a scavenger
so restless in your wakings
picking remnants in the hours
thieving at the doorstep

to sleep — this threshold
I trace your silhouette
mussed hair dark on grey
we are always touching

a careless limb a stray finger
ankles knees and elbows
the bread-warm stretch of you
chest beat like wings

slipping in and out
breaking surface tension
and my thoughts of you
a lasso made of motes.

A new lexicon

You are
the day that tastes like mango
a silver asterix on my night's page

We are
hyphenated-bifurcated
locked in a bolt of ampersand

you & me
subject and predicate
what you do to me

phonetically you're a bell chime
the wings of a hummingbird
shower drops on stained glass

as sense-making as the Oxford comma
a cathedral of silence
in a white noise world

you are the ascender
to my descender
boldly *italicised*

backwards and forwards
palindromatically
whichever way spelt

from contents to index
a fount of meaning you are
laid out crisply to read.

Enjambment

Esc to a new pg where
we speak the same language

Enter
there's no full stop

just a sliding
into the next line

Ctrl alt delete
if we make a blot

you can leave white spaces
and I can still read you.

Obverse

What shape would I have been
under different constellations
shaken like a snow dome
whittled and forged anew
by recombinant splices
of chance and catalyst?

What form would you have taken
were I not there to fire you
the many edges of a jewel
depend on how the light falls
whether the sunset is burnt sugar
or a bloodied heart in a bowl.

Pivot

My hair is the colour of space
you can get lost in it
dark star shining
to beguile into distraction

anything can prevail
between bloom and decay
birds with their steady oars
rowing downstream

fish flapping in the clouds
gills open to airy mists
and you at pivot point
between this world and the next.

Sofa Rock

There's a rock on the beach
hewn by forbears of cut crescents
& ravenously licked by tides
that cups both our bodies tight

hugging us in its gutted hollow
as your eyes make shapes
from slowly moving spun silk
and the lemon light falls on my face

into the crook of your collarbone
I'm shell-smoothed
soft-centred and stilled
silver trailing the line of you.

Ukiyo, The Floating World

Let's detach from after
sluice it off our skins
let the sweetness of now
season any tartness of then

your resting beside me
is measurable in units
like the green breath of forest
palpable and true

let's erase those hard lines
the exacting spreadsheet
that will pin us to the ground
anvilled to tomorrow

today we are amorphous
permeable and silky
dandelion-free and on the whim
of wind and birdsong

For you I would

fold the passage of time
into small portable squares
surrender kites from their strings
capture the heart of a geode

For you I would

rinse the dark sky clean
braid the air with veering eagles
harvest a wild red peony
cut through a field of sugarcane

For you I would

replace all lacunae
with hieroglyphics
score the stone of us
soft tuff until sheen.

Magnet

Fricative like a broken zip
this fabric of being alone
but I'm not chasing
I'm magnetic

you can come to me
after you've tramped the earth
stretched and shook
the poles between us

don't pretend
you don't miss me
surely you remember
the sun spilling on us

that I didn't need to drink
already carbonated and high
aerated with hope
and cordial stickiness

but now under a cataract sky
that hides you and blinds me
our tongues in mute
connective tissue taut

yet veined in golden floss
just know these pulses
undercurrent across oceans
are charged and unceasing.

Dark Blue

Wishing I could
unblue this heart
such shallowness
in the lung of life

no steely warrior
but a corpse pose
breath stuttering
in the red of life

to clasp my own hand
frigid in self-regard
walk without shadow
in the white of life.

Stet

What I would give
to kiss your heartbeat again
in tapping distance

to part your hair
a restless wave
the light dancing across

whispers on finger tips
this luxe sensitivity
of skin licked soothed

What I would give
to be vagabonds of the night
unbeholden to the end

to stand as we were before
defiant by default
suspended in this sentence.

Etymology

I may as well
construct a sieve
for the wandering stars

the chance I had
of holding onto us
yet our cartographies

are mapped within me
intersecting lines
blue and red

if I return there
ghost signs of you
remain on buildings

shrouded in paradox
of presence and absence
trailing our origin story.

Inside out

Feels like I ripped out my backbone
handed it over to you
a string of pearls you could wear
draped across your neck

and I am all skin
shed of fortitude and shame
just wanting you
to build me anew

come hither fingers
to lace up muscle and sinew
oxygenate the breathless
puppet me awake

Semaphore

1.
Even though I wrote
from candlewax
dripped from light
pink to squid ink

my poem
is a single note
square root multiplied
to the power of ten

2.
the way I lie at night
positioned just so
invisible semaphores
in outstretched fingers

a signalling on land
these flash code points
to be read over sea
over long-crested waves

3.
do you know of Janus words?
like when cleave
means both to join
and to cut apart

you're still here
but elsewhere
in defiance of all laws
because I hold the flags aloft.

SPACES

To be a Writer

First, why martyr yourself like this? —
a drive so masochistic & egotistic
why write about the sun
from the cool divide of your room?

consider: when you are moulting
like a deciduous maple
flaked-off skin on floorboards —
your hide has taken a beating

from pesky editors and gatekeepers
to glory and legacy and eternity
— you need quiet respite from the
pricks of rivals' blooming garlands

you have to bury the hatchet not the lede
be as versatile as a Dickinson dash —
ambidextrous in your politics
— and remember to have rich parents.

Apocalypse in the car park

1. Listen here Oscar

we may all be in the gutter
but some of us can't look at the stars:
cracked glasses awry so
rooted instead of sky eyed

shuffling among pebbles
grounded heel-blistered
there's virulence in the air
so shut your upbeat mouth

we're not swallowing your cheer
closed up impermeable
precarity the only sustenance
& the taste of trailing star dust.

2. Listen here Thomas

April is not the cruellest month
the preceding ones weren't exactly dandy
the ones in pursuit bloody clawed & toothed

we hold our collective breaths
& wonder, dear heart, what now?
do we have enough within us
to grieve in stoic columns?

not to writhe and sigh and loosen
the grit in stack by stack formation

so soft bellied we are to harbingers
of change of unrest of unknowing.

3. Desire Lines

Like the reach of Midas
the dying sun will sweep its gaze
over & turn you gold for me

because I can't do the touching
it will be my spread of hands
this gloss upon your shoulders

a softening of day's edge
these aureate filaments
desire lines to you.

4. Apocalypse in the car park

It's preternaturally calm
Hitchcockian seagulls malinger
in silent watchful pairs

off-peak cars crouch over
blunt-wheeled trolleys
& dusk's palette is deepening

everywhere eyes averted
hands under surveillance:
aliens are in the slipstream.

Weltschmerz

We are now boneless
trying to remember how to regrow
limbs and organs
staring at the dead black eye
in the centre of the room

the script keeps changing:
do we exit left or slip down the pothole?
honeycombed in our apartments
so industrious with the knitting
of time slipped with loose knots.

Chrysos

1. After

When all this is over
I want to take your hand and run
into forest into city into sea
I want to rip apart this fabric
filming over our eyes
blow all dandelion florets
into the green and chase them
holler and cause violence to silence
careen into corners tumble like marbles
down hillocks spiderwebs brushing
I want to loiter with no intent
in alcoves mischief-making
and exhale to the sun.

2. Wayfinding

If only there was another exit
except the one through the gift store

and crows actually flew in straight lines
not in great wheeling arcs

if only the moonlit flip of silvery koi
taught us how to swim upstream

and sign posts were sign language
gesticulations in mid-air flurry

cutting through labyrinthine
paths right to the heart.

3. Wabi-sabi

There won't be any deus ex machina
swooping down to save us fools
theatrical in the bustle of life business
so smug in schedules and shopping
tomorrow and tomorrow and tomorrow
we thought, so righteous and sure
but now coughing, ashen and circumspect
felled by our own dirty hands
so best not to look to the heavens
time to divest space & remain still
be a witness not a player
practice insider art, exhale in solitude.

4. Chrysos

On our knees and atrophied
how do we recall the muscle memory
of rolling in green-sea grass?
how do we scrape the walls of life
to find the seams of gold?

soon we'll part the curtains
whose bold print had bleached in the sun
when time moved so sedulously
we'll stretch the perimeters of our bodies
ephemerality in this earth hurtling us on.

Melbourne in concert

1. Let's meet beneath the clocks I say you know the usual steps fourth
row from the top I'll be leaning against the slightly sticky rail the
weak glare of autumnal sun contouring my face gazing across the vista
of shapes of billboards of buildings horizontal and vertical and jagged
the crane on its downward pendulum with religion-commerce-
entertainment captured within lazy eye-sweep looming over swarming
pedestrians such shoals of industry the cars-trams-bikes a hubbub of
noise neon flash traffic light tick tick in concert with hoots of careless
laughter with food pimps promise of 20 percent off vegan curry and
the righteous dude with hand-scribbled placard to save our souls
and over there designer goths fishnets-slashed eyeliner-scowled and
over here salarymen in hermetic bubbles of importance pushing past
leisurewear mums ferrying the next generation a smear of chocolate
as thick as blood across baby cheeks and upwards a stray balloon
bouncing and downwards hardened balls of gum underfoot and on
the right bouquets for the nose and the tableaux of moving images
roll on and on in continuous loop but then a shrill in the ear as you
say hey the Sunbury line is running late again.

2. Let's meet at the cafe around the corner you know the one where
the actor-barista has a python wrapped 'round his bicep and always
tries to flirt with me and sniggers at you behind his lumberjack
beard about your weak decaf order why even bother mate fine you
stick with your lukewarm brown bath-water I need a strong double
hit need to stay awake for that bar I was telling you about past the
graffitied alley down that cobbled laneway behind the dumpster of
course there's no visible signage don't be silly we have to look both
cool and desperate and wait for the mixologist to peek behind the
heavy drapes take pity and invite us inside me in a backless sparkly
number you gelled and cufflinked nonchalantly welcomed into the
gloom into the glittery decadence low-key ambient tones bouncing

off the black gloss cut sharp I want to sink into those luxe red velvet booths sip cocktails with names of German Expressionist actresses blink at the slowly revolving disco ball then close my eyes altogether feel the frisson of you near me your fingertips trailing my arm the deliciousness of it heat and touch and heat and touch.

3. Let's meet under the arches where little firefly lights are already shimmering in the gloaming and the lanterns are bobbing in the goosepimply breeze did you know that my favourite colour is red did you know that this is the longest Chinese settlement in the western world of course you don't too busy checking out every bubble cup tea shop on the strip yeah I know your usual order milky taro with pearls and jelly I may have a durian ice-cream instead so over sneers of its week-old socks scent I mean no one has a swipe about stinky French cheeses do they but first let's go get us some dumplings and green tea and something crispy and salty and just pick a place already past those white marble lions with roars petrified and those cheongsam smiley lures fanning themselves with half-chewed menus I want sesame sizzle and you can have fire engine-bright chillies with your stir-fry doused with an Asahi or Bingtang let's try a noodle house maybe honeyed prawns tossed on the side water spinach in spicy shrimp paste and can we go visit a herbalist grocery store after I need some Tiger balm my back is killing me.

4. Let's meet beneath the water wall look I've found a veiny tri-coloured leaf to stick on it place your hands there yeah like that so cool hey stop flicking me c'mon no past the gift shop we can do that later let's go to the permanents the oils and the drawings the glass and the solids the wisp of dreams by those of bygone eras the chutzpah of the moderns form and chaos let's zig-zag back and forth and get lost in the labyrinthine corridors and be spooked out by all those

canvas eyes following us across cavernous rooms then we can lie on
the carpet unravelling but fingers entwined beneath the hard-edged
tapestry ceiling our eyes awash with colour just shake your head
gently side by side it's a kaleidoscope a dazzle to fill ourselves up with
wonder later I have opening tickets to a show next door at the mini
spire the venue where 75,000 tiny brass cups are on the ceiling yup
that many we can dress up and saunter along the plush carpet and
gold gilt and then after cross the upside-down river check out the
flotsam of movement swirling in the purple dark.

5. Let's meet at the tram stop in front of the library no don't drive in
you know how hopeless you are at hook turns just PT it if you don't
see me I'll be chatting to *The Big Issue* vendor at his usual corner or
throwing a few coins to the busker but really I'd rather just pay him
to stop butchering The Stones already c'mon we have time can dawdle
window shop a little do you know the French term for that literally
means licking windows so true we can't afford any of that stuff just
stick our tongues out in abject desire let's flaneur with lazy detours
down to the Tan instead down to the ornamental lake there past
the 3,000 succulents all spiky and fleshy and small red yellow pink
flowering let's find a spot on the green beneath the green you can
read me another chapter of that book you have to do all the accents
I'll lay my head on your lap shutter my flicking eyes listen to your
voice to the murmuring breeze to the faraway buzz of traffic.

Hyphenated

Cognitive dissonance is an Asian woman
who has to carry her grandmother's special phở
in her lukewarm blood to impress at dinner parties,
be after-schooled in strings and numbers:
a hothouse orchid with no outside breeze

she has to be an ingenue unwise to the ways of men
who largely want her for her smallness
the wriggling cheongsam the flutter fingers
then stillness: bamboo waist and water lily serene
lickable caramel against their burly chests

everyone loves a happy migrant story:
leaky prawn trawler to valedictorian
a seam of jade trapped in ancestral dust
to be extracted and rubbed to sheen
she has to blaze a trail to prove she's keen.

Milk

Not whitewashing my name
means I have to proffer a new one
so the barista can call out
something pale and watery
like half-strength English breakfast
to wash down the fluffy scones
made from full cream
homogenised milk.

How to make your heart beat

Something inside of me cracked open
and I let you step inside
the glistening yolk of it all
dripped through my fingers

in the quiet parts of me
you are there bolted down
a furry pelt against my cheek
such staunchness in the night

to make your heart beat
you don't need much:
sea glass in the palm
half moons in thumbnails

pearling drops of blood
cirrused across water
the skies underbellied with cloud:
waiting like an epigraph.

Found object

I want someone I can turn into art
splice him into shapes
assemble him again:
    slightly askew

I want to impasto his body
into thick strokes
lather on the touch;
    textured wetly

I want to rinse out his eyes
replace with cyan
drips from a sharp nib:
    pinpointed deep

I want to Baroque him in gold leaf
all fired shimmery
theatre in repose:
    gilded in heat

I want Pollock impulses
tenderised by water lilies
a soul on virgin canvas
        stretched taut

I want someone I can turn into art
stencilled with precision
and my name a smeary triumph
        on the bottom right corner.

Out of Water

1. A mauve wash rinsed the sky
& the sun lazily undressed
as you walked me through
the contrary weather of yourself:
thunderclaps and aridity

your words rolled in tune
to the flux of river
& the murmur of concert
Such Sophoclean vigour:
the dramas of your heart

and I, a chorus of one
curled up on the bench
head angled to catch the drops
flavoured sharp and acidic
that have devoured you so

2. With a constellation of lights
both natural and mannered
contouring us in the dim
the goosebumps on your skin
braille I can fluently read

the universal language of despair
& the labours of redemption:
your voice a silvery fish flipping
above the sounds of industry and music
you are exposed to the air.

but the chorus of one sings out
with reminders of agency and trust
of beauty and of mending
with stitches by another hand
of a new turn around the sun.

Dégustation

I want to show you
the pulse of the city
at eventide

opening nights on velvet
blood red to sink into
the whiteness of your throat

profiled against the plush
cheekbones cut sharp
senses carried away

by the vibrato
the genuflection
the arabesque

glitter fictions on stage
more urgent & assailable
than any mere life hurt

later in front of canvas
the squalls of colour and shape
laid out for dégustation

then skin chilled like wine
I want you to bend and kiss
the heavy petals of my eyelids.

Kitchen sink melodrama

You: all black, pacing the room [*slowly because injured physically/
psychically]
Me: dishevelled. wrap dress & hair awry

Both of us: coming apart after coming together (almost)
Torrents rushing from your mouth

Me: confused
You: apologetic

I want to touch you
you are unravelling at the seams

[still life tableau] statuesque grey cat in corner in disgust; half eaten
containers of Thai, doughnuts in piecemeal

Outside: A drizzle tease

A Pinter Pause

.

Exit Scene 1.

****

Later. Scene 11.

By my car: white in the gloom

You: barefoot on wet tarmac. Slightly wild. Rushes from your mouth
now a trickle

Me: I still want to touch you. Hold you so tight that all your invisible leakages will seal

Both of us: a matrix of chaos

The sky: let's just open now. Yes. Right now
[heavy, heavy rain]

[unheard but inferred: low orchestral strings]

The sound of a car slowly pulling away from the kerb

Red tail lights flash.

Close.

Hermes

I want to feel the surge of your body the metronome beat the heat
of you fingernail close I want to lick my lips and place them on you
every vertebra arched ready a wet clutch hold on you

but it's so precious the China cabinet of your heart you are high wire
tripping assailed caged beige raging then chloroformed numb tears
waterfalling down your face ineffably away from me

I write poems of sand to slip through the cracks of you harden like
cement stop the crumbling to soothe to smooth a flannel to your
zealous forehead with oils reaped from the benevolent earth

I write lest the cave of night swallows you lest you wrest with
phantoms lashed to a Turner mast bilious coloured in your cheeks

just to see you blue sky Summer holidays frangipani sweet healthy
brain veined my pen it can grow wings like Hermes fly to you.

Gifts for buoyancy

1. In the tea-black sea
    you're adrenalin-lashed
    gasping for a future island
    the ballast in the loll and lull?
    an exultation of larks above

    imagine: our whipped sheets
    currents to the shore
    my arm across your chest
    sinuous as a swan neck
    sea breath in your ear

2. I'd like to gift you
    a book of flames
    combustible on receipt
    a promise of unmaking
    to raze you shooting green

    a bowerbird scrupulous
    in hoarding memories
    of small embers of radiance
    & fistfuls of red grevilleas
    energy charged by the sun.

Synchronicity

Waiting for the moment/when my tag is graffitied/glow in the dark/
dragonfly neon/lapidary swirls across the flat plane of your back

the point where/stormwater heart/banked up for weeks/now at the
fingertip/a meniscus of raindrop/curved like crystal

where Rorschach clouds/nebulous/in rosewater sky/wisps slowly knit
together/a mandala/portents/of synchronicity

later in dove-grey light/I am waiting/for trees to grow pages/I can
write on/criss-cross the days in tiny black marks/ant trails to you.

Serenade

Beneath a moon fed fat with cream
dead stars blinking of the past
I dance with you in my dream

A hand cuts sharp through the air
the strings and woodwork stir from rest
beneath a moon fed fat with cream

arrayed in velvet petal folds
swaying red to the heartbeat
I dance with you in my dream

with the dull streets now alight
polished smooth in the rain
beneath a moon fed fat with cream

the Doric elegance of you
speaking to me through skin
I dance with you in my dream.

Green colony

Slowly they are taking over
the monstera the pothos
the one that's impossibly round
others jagged and defensive
in corners half-lit
motes falling in the gloom
in iris-contracting brightness
self-watering righteousness
whispering language you're yet to read:
 a surfeit a lack
liquid light heat
all of us breathing green
fronds trembling
curlicues colonising
stalks that salute the sun
a contagion of scent
our lungs so full.

Warming the apartment

About six months now:
you have a favourite stove top
know precisely when the solar fairy lights
would glow-worm across the balcony

how the sun sets just so
skimming tree tops
a contour of blush edging
a palette that draws the birds to roost

you can assign dogs to barks unseen
sleep to goodnight kisses of traffic
grow books in corners like mushrooms
cultivate louche self-governance

let the dishes gather in a melee
offer amnesty to hairline cracks
usurp patriarchal decrees:
wallow in your own fiefdom.

Tomorrow: to Ava

I bequeath you
newspaper fingers:
my life's work in columns
to see truth in fiction

I beseech you
to carry always a question:
be weaponised against absolutes
argue and bluster and rail

I expect you to fall
to your knees
wet-eyed and humbled
a rag tossed in the wind

I want you to drape
my favourite word
across your shoulders
like an amulet:

serendipity
this blessing for
karmic restitution
a fortune's wheel re-spun

I offer you
time travel and tomorrow building
to see what was then
is an elastic stretch of now

petrichor from drying grass
cherry blossoms on bitumen
fernweh and *komorebi*
aestheticism unto itself

I   to   you
all   the   in   be   tween
spaces   to   fill

A room of one's own

See how the chambers swell
accordionised

stoked up by the bellows
there is room

an indulgence stretched
wider for being alone

outside there is reach
a grapefruit horizon

flowers like trumpets
heralding

day hidden stars
the choreography of starlings

I can trace with a finger
sky writing my name.

Art for art's sake

Those paper cuts
outside of tradition
Pater and Wilde and Swinburne

degenerates in the service of words:
it's not utilitarian not a bridge
your soul will not be higher learned

a poem is not moral fibre
washed down with holy water
taken with a grimace

exempt from the body politic
its charm lies in its charm
an anathema to rectitude

just as Beardsley's curiosities
in those black and white lines
are to be swooned over ecstatically

all art is quite useless
to be lived beautifully
a flower unfurls for itself.

ACKNOWLEDGEMENTS

Thank you to the team at UWAP, who once again took on my poetry manuscript and transformed it into a thing of beauty, and to Creative Victoria, who offered me a Creative Workers Fund that helped me buy time to work on *Decadence*.

Thanks also to my family, friends and other cheerleaders, in particular: Ava Milne, Maria Takolander, Maxine Beneba Clarke, Andy Jackson, Joanne Vizzari, David Nichols, Vicki Renner, Melanie Schwarz, Jackie Tang, Raphaelle Race, Emma Hegarty, George Papadopoulos, Leanne Stanczyk, Rahne Widarsito, Mandy Beaumont, Anna Solding, Leila Lois, Vanessa Francesca, Brent Turner and David 'Dorian' Rule.

Poems in *Decadence* have previously been published in the following:

'A New Lexicon' was published in Writers Victoria, *The Victorian Writer*, June-Sept 'Sense and Sensibilities' 2020 edition.

'Chrysos' suite of poems was published online in Multicultural Arts Victoria's Shelter Project.

'Apocalypse in the car park' suite of poems was published in *The Moth* magazine, Autumn 2020 edition.

'Prelude', 'Williamstown Pier' and 'Bird-boned' were published online in *Eureka Street* magazine.

'Hyphenated' was published online in 'Brownface' edition of *Cordite* and also in the *Best Of Australian Poems* 2021.

'Wide open road' was shortlisted in November 2020's 'Freedom' flash writing competition in Writing from the Heart.

'26 Soldiers', 'Milk', 'L'espirit l'escalier', 'Enjambment', and 'Symphony' were published in *The Saturday Paper* on 20 February 2021.

'26 Soldiers' was also published in *Australian Poetry*, Volume 9 2021–2022.

'Word slut' was published in Writers Victoria newsletter, *The Victorian Writer* March-May 2021 Wordsmith edition.

A snippet of 'Bonsai Clipped' was featured in the Raining Poetry in Adelaide Festival 2021.

An excerpt of 'Melbourne in concert' (under the name 'Melbourne Symphony') was featured with accompanying illustration in Melbourne's City Square as part of the MWF/Metro Tunnel project: 'Writing Melbourne.'

'Decadence', 'Lasso' and 'For you I would' have been published in *Eureka Street*.

'Get Lit' has been shortlisted in the Ada Cambridge Prize 2021 as part of the Williamstown Literary Festival.